PRINCEWILL LAGANG

Parenting as Partners: Navigating Parenthood Together

First published by PRINCEWILL LAGANG 2023

Copyright © 2023 by Princewill Lagang

All rights reserved. No part of this publication may be reproduced, stored or transmitted in any form or by any means, electronic, mechanical, photocopying, recording, scanning, or otherwise without written permission from the publisher. It is illegal to copy this book, post it to a website, or distribute it by any other means without permission.

Princewill Lagang asserts the moral right to be identified as the author of this work.

First edition

This book was professionally typeset on Reedsy.
Find out more at reedsy.com

Contents

1	Introduction	1
2	Redefining Parenthood as a Partnership	3
3	Effective Communication in Parenting	6
4	Aligning Parenting Styles	9
5	Building a Strong Parenting Foundation	12
6	Supporting Each Other's Well-being	15
7	Division of Parenting Roles	18
8	Parenting Through Challenges	21
9	Fostering Individuality in Children	23
10	Navigating Extended Family Dynamics	25
11	Maintaining Intimacy as Partners and Parents	27
12	Growing Together as Parents and Partners	30

1

Introduction

Parenthood as a Collaborative Journey: Embracing the Power of Teamwork

In the realm of raising children, a profound shift is underway - a transformation in the traditional understanding of parenting. Gone are the days when one parent assumed the role of the stern disciplinarian while the other played the nurturing caregiver. The dynamics of modern family life have given rise to a new paradigm: parenting as a partnership. This book embarks on a journey to explore the significance of teamwork in parenting and how it has become an indispensable cornerstone of effective child-rearing.

In an era where dual-income households are the norm and gender roles are evolving, the concept of parenting as a partnership has taken center stage. No longer can the responsibilities of raising children be shouldered by a single individual. The demands of contemporary life have illuminated the necessity for parents to forge a cooperative alliance, where their strengths and weaknesses complement each other. The traditional notions of "mom" and "dad" have transcended into a shared endeavor, where the collective efforts of both parents steer the family ship.

But why is teamwork so crucial in this voyage of parenting? As we navigate the challenges of nurturing and guiding the next generation, it becomes evident that a harmonious partnership enhances the quality of upbringing. Collaborative parenting not only disperses the workload but also nurtures an environment of emotional support and understanding. Children flourish when they witness their parents working together, fostering an atmosphere of unity and respect.

Throughout the chapters of this book, we will delve into the various dimensions of this collaborative parenting approach. We will explore how effective communication, division of responsibilities, and mutual decision-making can create a solid foundation for the growth and development of our children. Real-life anecdotes and expert insights will illuminate the rewards and intricacies of this transformative parenting paradigm.

As we embark on this journey, it is crucial to remember that while the concept of parenting as a partnership is an ideal to strive for, it is not without its challenges. Balancing careers, personal aspirations, and family commitments can be daunting. Nonetheless, the benefits of such a partnership far outweigh the difficulties. By embracing this evolving role of parenthood, we equip ourselves with the tools to raise resilient, empathetic, and well-rounded individuals.

So, let us embark on this exploration together, as we uncover the art of collaborative parenting and celebrate the strength that emerges when two individuals unite to raise a child. In the chapters that follow, we will dissect the principles, share practical strategies, and celebrate the victories that result from embracing parenting as a partnership.

2

Redefining Parenthood as a Partnership

Shifting from Solitude to Synergy: The Evolution of Collaborative Parenting

In the annals of history, the roles of mothers and fathers within the family unit were often distinct and well-defined. Mothers were the primary nurturers, responsible for the emotional needs of the children, while fathers assumed the role of breadwinners and disciplinarians. However, societal changes, gender equality movements, and the evolving dynamics of family life have given rise to a transformative shift in the way we perceive parenthood. This chapter explores the metamorphosis from traditional parental roles to the dynamic landscape of collaborative parenting.

Gone are the days of isolated motherhood or fatherhood, where one parent bore the weight of the parenting journey. The dawn of collaborative parenting is upon us, encouraging parents to come together as equal partners, sharing the joys and challenges of child-rearing. This shift is not merely a change in semantics, but a fundamental restructuring of the way parents engage with their children and each other. It's a move from unilateral decisions to joint choices, from segmented responsibilities to shared endeavors.

Central to this transformation is the idea of sharing responsibilities. Collaborative parenting recognizes that the emotional, physical, and intellectual needs of children are best met when both parents actively participate. By redistributing tasks and duties, parents can create a more balanced family environment, ensuring that no burden falls disproportionately on one individual. From diaper changes to bedtime stories, the act of sharing in the daily routines fosters a sense of unity and mutual support.

Equally significant is the concept of joint decision-making. Traditional parenting often relied on a hierarchical approach, where one parent held the final say in matters concerning the children. However, collaborative parenting promotes an open exchange of ideas, where both parents contribute to decisions that impact their family. This not only allows for a broader range of perspectives but also teaches children the value of compromise, negotiation, and respect for diverse viewpoints.

The benefits of this collaborative approach are multifold. Children grow up witnessing a partnership built on respect and cooperation, laying the groundwork for healthy relationships in their own lives. Moreover, as parents learn to communicate effectively and compromise willingly, the overall harmony of the household improves, creating an environment conducive to growth and learning.

But, as with any transformation, challenges can arise. Balancing work, personal aspirations, and parental duties requires careful navigation. The expectations and biases of society may sometimes clash with the ideals of collaborative parenting. Nonetheless, the rewards of this approach are well worth the effort. It's a journey that embarks on the principle that when parents unite their strengths and work in tandem, the result is not only a more fulfilling parenting experience but also children who are better equipped to navigate the complexities of the world.

In the chapters ahead, we will explore strategies for effective collaboration, delve into real-life stories of parents who have successfully embraced this approach, and uncover the ways in which the essence of partnership can transform the art of raising children. As we journey forward, let us continue to redefine parenthood as a partnership, embracing its challenges and celebrating its triumphs.

3

Effective Communication in Parenting

Building Bridges of Understanding: Navigating Parenthood Through Open Dialogue

In the intricate web of collaborative parenting, effective communication stands as the cornerstone of success. The ability for partners to engage in open, honest, and respectful conversations lays the foundation for a harmonious parenting journey. This chapter delves into the vital role of communication in co-parenting, providing strategies for discussing parenting goals, concerns, and decisions, fostering an environment of trust and understanding.

At the heart of collaborative parenting lies the notion that both partners bring unique perspectives, experiences, and insights to the table. To harness the power of this diversity, open communication is essential. Partners must create a safe space where they can express their thoughts, concerns, and aspirations without fear of judgment. By listening attentively and without interruption, they not only validate each other's feelings but also foster a sense of mutual respect.

A key element in effective communication is active listening. This involves not just hearing the words spoken, but also understanding the emotions and intentions behind them. Empathetic listening allows partners to truly grasp each other's viewpoints, enabling them to work together in making informed decisions. Such understanding paves the way for compromise and collaboration, essential components of successful co-parenting.

To initiate discussions, consider setting aside regular times for open dialogues. These conversations can revolve around short-term goals, long-term aspirations, or immediate concerns. Creating a structure provides a framework for addressing important topics and ensures that both partners are on the same page. Remember, consistency is key; even when discussions are challenging, the act of engaging in open dialogue strengthens the partnership.

When navigating through conversations about parenting decisions, it's crucial to maintain a solution-oriented mindset. Instead of dwelling on disagreements, focus on finding common ground and working together to address the issue at hand. Compromise might mean blending elements of both partners' viewpoints to create a solution that benefits the family as a whole. Through these negotiations, children witness firsthand the power of collaboration and problem-solving.

Respectful communication also extends to the ways in which partners provide feedback and offer suggestions. Constructive criticism, delivered with kindness and empathy, fosters an environment where both partners feel comfortable sharing their thoughts without apprehension. This approach encourages growth and learning for both individuals, enhancing their parenting skills and their relationship.

As with any skill, effective communication in parenting requires practice. It's a journey of continuous learning, self-awareness, and adaptation. Partners may find it valuable to attend workshops, read books, or seek professional guidance to refine their communication techniques. Remember, the goal is not to eliminate disagreements but to navigate them with respect, ensuring that they become opportunities for growth rather than sources of conflict.

In the subsequent chapters, we will explore scenarios that demand effective communication, ranging from managing challenging behaviors to discussing significant life changes. As we continue to unravel the intricacies of collaborative parenting, let us embrace the art of communication as a means to nurture our partnership, empower our children, and create a household filled with understanding and compassion.

4

Aligning Parenting Styles

Harmonizing Diverse Paths: Navigating Parenting Styles as a United Front

In the voyage of collaborative parenting, the waters can sometimes become turbulent when partners bring distinct parenting styles to the table. These styles, often shaped by personal experiences, cultural backgrounds, and beliefs, may vary significantly. This chapter embarks on a journey to explore the art of aligning parenting styles, understanding the differences, and finding common ground to create a unified approach to raising children.

Parenting styles are like unique maps guiding the course of how parents interact with and nurture their children. Traditional models include authoritative, permissive, and authoritarian styles, each characterized by its own set of values and principles. When partners possess different styles, there is potential for conflicts to arise, and children might receive inconsistent messages.

Navigating these differences starts with understanding and appreciating the origins of each partner's parenting style. Open dialogue about their upbringing, cultural influences, and beliefs can illuminate the reasons behind their approaches. This understanding can provide a bridge to empathy and compassion, fostering an environment where both partners acknowledge the validity of each other's perspectives.

To find common ground, it's essential to identify shared values and overarching goals for the upbringing of your children. By focusing on what you both want to achieve – such as instilling values, fostering independence, or promoting emotional well-being – partners can begin to weave a cohesive parenting fabric. This shared vision becomes a guiding light when making decisions about discipline, routines, and other aspects of child-rearing.

Conflicts arising from differing parenting styles can be opportunities for growth. Approach these disagreements with respect and curiosity, aiming to learn from each other rather than imposing your viewpoint. It's vital to remember that while individual approaches may differ, the underlying intention is often the same: the well-being and development of your children.

The key to a harmonious parenting partnership is to create a united front. This means presenting a consistent and aligned front to your children, even if you have different styles. Disagreements should be addressed privately, away from the children's presence. By doing so, children learn the importance of collaboration, compromise, and the value of respectful communication.

Over time, as partners continue to refine their parenting styles, there may be opportunities to blend elements from both approaches. Flexibility is crucial, as the needs of children evolve with time and circumstances. Adaptation demonstrates to children that growth is a continuous journey, and that learning from each other can lead to stronger bonds and enhanced parenting skills.

In the chapters ahead, we will explore scenarios that demand a unified approach to parenting, including discipline, education, and managing conflict.

As we delve deeper into the nuances of collaborative parenting, let us celebrate the diversity in our styles while striving to create a harmonious symphony, where every note contributes to the growth and development of our children.

5

Building a Strong Parenting Foundation

Forging a Unified Path: Shared Values and Consistency in Parenting

In the realm of collaborative parenting, a solid foundation is paramount for navigating the complexities of raising children. This chapter delves into the pivotal importance of establishing shared values and goals as parents, and how this foundation serves as the bedrock for creating a united front, ensuring consistency in discipline, guidance, and decision-making.

Shared values and goals act as the North Star guiding parents through the intricate journey of child-rearing. By aligning on fundamental principles, partners create a roadmap for their parenting endeavors. Begin by identifying the core values you want to instill in your children – be it empathy, respect, curiosity, or resilience. These values serve as touchstones, helping parents make decisions that align with their collective aspirations.

Engage in open discussions about your long-term goals as parents. What kind of individuals do you hope your children will become? How do you envision their emotional well-being and growth? Establishing a shared vision not only strengthens your partnership but also ensures that both partners contribute to the shaping of your children's lives.

A united front is crucial for maintaining consistency in discipline and guidance. Children are skilled at identifying differences in their parents' approaches, and inconsistency can lead to confusion and manipulation. Whether it's enforcing rules, setting boundaries, or addressing misbehavior, presenting a unified front demonstrates to your children that both parents stand together in their decisions.

One effective strategy for establishing a unified front is to have regular conversations about parenting matters. Share your observations, experiences, and concerns, and work together to create a consistent approach. Discuss potential scenarios and decide in advance how you will handle them, so you're both prepared to respond cohesively in the moment.

When disagreements arise, approach them with respect and empathy. Rather than engaging in power struggles, consider the impact your decisions will have on your children's development. Keep the shared values and goals in mind, and explore compromises that allow you both to maintain your alignment as parents.

Consistency in discipline and guidance also extends to communication with your children. Presenting a united front ensures that your messages are clear and coherent. If one parent makes a decision, the other should support it, even if there are differing opinions behind closed doors. Over time, children will come to understand that the family operates as a team, and that their parents' decisions are rooted in shared values.

As we navigate the complexities of collaborative parenting, let us remember that a strong foundation is essential for smooth sailing. By establishing shared values and goals, we provide our children with a nurturing environment where they can thrive. By presenting a united front, we equip ourselves to address challenges with consistency and empathy. In the upcoming chapters, we will delve into real-life scenarios where a strong parenting foundation proves invaluable, showing us the transformative power of a partnership built on shared aspirations.

6

Supporting Each Other's Well-being

Nurturing Ourselves, Nurturing Our Partnership: The Interplay of Individual and Collective Well-being in Collaborative Parenting

In the symphony of collaborative parenting, the individual notes of partners' well-being harmonize to create a resonant melody that echoes through the household. This chapter delves into the essential practice of balancing self-care while also supporting each other's emotional needs. As we explore the interplay between personal well-being and effective parenting, we discover how nurturing ourselves contributes to the strength of our partnership.

Amid the myriad responsibilities of parenthood, it's crucial to remember that partners are also individuals with unique needs and aspirations. Balancing the demands of parenting with self-care is not a luxury, but a necessity. Prioritizing your well-being enables you to bring your best self to the partnership and parenting journey. By carving out time for activities that rejuvenate and energize you, you model healthy self-care practices for your children.

Supporting each other's well-being is an act of compassion and partnership. Recognize and acknowledge the stressors your partner faces, whether they stem from parenting, work, or other aspects of life. Listen actively and offer your understanding and empathy. This support fosters a sense of connection, reinforcing the partnership's strength and creating an environment where both partners feel valued.

Effective parenting as partners requires us to recognize the interconnectedness of our well-being. When one partner is struggling, it can ripple through the family dynamic. Thus, nurturing each other's well-being becomes an investment in the family's happiness and stability. A partnership built on empathy and mutual support not only creates a harmonious household but also equips children with valuable life skills.

Practicing self-care and supporting each other's well-being also enables us to model healthy behavior for our children. When children witness their parents taking time for themselves and supporting each other, they learn the importance of self-respect, empathy, and maintaining a balanced life. This foundation of well-being prepares them for their own journeys of growth and self-discovery.

A crucial aspect of supporting well-being is effective communication. Partners should openly discuss their needs, boundaries, and the types of support they require. Whether it's sharing household responsibilities, allowing space for personal hobbies, or planning regular breaks, clear communication ensures that both partners' needs are acknowledged and met.

In the chapters ahead, we will explore the ways in which self-care and emotional support contribute to the overall strength of collaborative parenting. From managing stress to fostering emotional resilience in children, the practices we cultivate in nurturing our individual well-being create a ripple effect that enriches our partnership and family life. Let us remember that by nurturing ourselves, we nurture our partnership, and by nurturing our partnership, we provide our children with a secure and nurturing environment to flourish.

7

Division of Parenting Roles

Harmonizing the Dance: Practical Strategies for Dividing Parenting Responsibilities

In the grand choreography of collaborative parenting, the division of parenting roles is a delicate art that requires balance, communication, and adaptability. This chapter delves into the practical ways partners can divide parenting responsibilities, ensuring that both partners contribute to the upbringing of their children while maintaining a sense of equilibrium within their partnership.

Effective division of parenting roles is rooted in recognizing each partner's strengths, preferences, and availability. Begin by having an open conversation about your respective work schedules, commitments, and personal interests. Identify tasks that align with each partner's strengths and preferences, creating a natural flow in the way responsibilities are shared.

Consider creating a parenting responsibilities chart that outlines tasks and routines. This chart can encompass everything from meal planning and bedtime routines to school pickups and extracurricular activities. Regularly review and adjust the chart as your children grow and circumstances change. Flexibility is key; the demands of parenting evolve, and your division of roles should reflect those changes.

Partners should strive for equality in the distribution of responsibilities, taking into account both the quantity and the nature of tasks. Equality, however, does not always mean a perfect 50/50 split; it means finding a balance that suits the dynamics of your partnership and your individual capacities. Flexibility is essential, as certain situations may require one partner to take on more responsibilities temporarily.

Maintaining open lines of communication is crucial for a successful division of parenting roles. Regularly check in with each other to ensure that both partners feel supported and valued. Discuss any challenges that arise, and be open to adjusting your approach based on your children's needs and your evolving partnership.

As children grow and their needs change, roles may naturally shift. What worked when they were toddlers might not be suitable for their teenage years. Be willing to adapt and make changes as necessary, demonstrating to your children the importance of flexibility and collaboration in managing family dynamics.

It's important to remember that dividing parenting responsibilities isn't just about tasks; it's about creating a cohesive family unit where both partners contribute to the physical and emotional well-being of the children. When children see their parents working together and supporting each other, they learn valuable lessons about partnership, cooperation, and effective time management.

In the upcoming chapters, we will explore how the division of parenting roles impacts different aspects of family life, from maintaining a balanced household to managing extracurricular activities. By nurturing a partnership that balances responsibilities and adapts to change, we create an environment where both parents and children thrive, each contributing their unique strengths to the intricate dance of collaborative parenting.

8

Parenting Through Challenges

Navigating Stormy Seas: Strategies for Overcoming Challenges as a United Parenting Team

The journey of collaborative parenting is not without its storms. Challenges arise in various forms, from sleepless nights and work-life balance struggles to behavioral issues that test our patience. This chapter dives into the art of parenting through challenges, offering strategies for partners to face difficulties as a united team and emerge stronger on the other side.

Sleep deprivation, a common challenge in early parenting, can strain even the strongest partnerships. Begin by openly discussing your sleep schedules and finding ways to share nighttime responsibilities. Establish a routine that provides both partners with adequate rest, ensuring that neither feels overwhelmed by the demands of caregiving.

Work-life balance is another hurdle that many parents face. Partners should communicate openly about their work commitments and strive to create a balance that allows for quality family time. Prioritize activities that recharge your energy and nurture your relationship, whether it's a family outing, a date night, or a simple evening of shared relaxation.

Behavioral issues can be particularly challenging, testing the patience and unity of parents. When faced with these challenges, partners should present a united front. Collaboratively define rules, consequences, and methods of discipline. Agree on how to respond to specific behaviors, maintaining a consistent approach to avoid confusion for your children.

In moments of frustration, it's essential to remember that you are a team. Support each other emotionally and offer a listening ear. Avoid blaming or criticizing, and instead seek solutions together. Remember that every challenge presents an opportunity for growth and learning, both individually and as a partnership.

One effective strategy is to establish a "parenting huddle" – a regular check-in where you discuss challenges, successes, and strategies for handling specific situations. This proactive approach ensures that both partners are on the same page and strengthens the sense of partnership in addressing parenting challenges.

During challenging times, practicing self-compassion is crucial. Remember that it's okay to ask for help, whether from each other, family members, or professionals. Seek advice from trusted sources, attend parenting workshops, or consider counseling if needed. Demonstrating a willingness to learn and adapt models resilience for your children.

In the chapters ahead, we will explore specific challenges that collaborative parenting might encounter, offering strategies and insights to navigate each situation. By approaching these challenges as a united team, you demonstrate to your children the power of partnership, empathy, and effective problem-solving. Through the storms and calms, remember that every challenge is an opportunity to strengthen your bond and enrich the tapestry of collaborative parenting.

9

Fostering Individuality in Children

Nurturing Unique Blossoms: Cultivating Children's Identities in a Collaborative Partnership

In the garden of collaborative parenting, one of the most beautiful flowers to cultivate is the individuality of each child. This chapter delves into the art of fostering individuality in children, exploring how partners can work together to encourage their children's unique interests, talents, and personalities while providing a nurturing environment for growth.

Every child is a masterpiece, painted with unique colors of interests, talents, and personalities. Encouraging their individuality is not only a celebration of their uniqueness but also a pathway to their personal growth and happiness. Partners can start by observing and listening to their children, discovering what lights up their eyes and brings joy to their hearts.

Supporting children's interests requires open communication between partners. Share observations and discuss how you can collectively provide opportunities for your children to explore their passions. Whether it's enrolling them in art classes, supporting their interest in science, or fostering their love for sports, a united front ensures that your children feel encouraged and valued.

Celebrating individuality also involves acknowledging and embracing differences in your children's personalities. One child might be outgoing and sociable, while another might be more introspective. Partners should work together to create an environment where both children feel accepted and appreciated for who they are.

Collaborative parenting allows for a balance between nurturing children's individuality and instilling shared values. Open conversations about your family's core values provide a compass for guiding your children's decisions and actions. As partners, you can ensure that the pursuit of personal passions aligns with the family's overarching principles.

Nurturing individuality requires providing a safe space for your children to express themselves. Encourage open conversations where your children feel comfortable sharing their thoughts and feelings. This practice strengthens the parent-child bond, creating a foundation of trust that allows them to confidently explore their interests.

Remember that fostering individuality is not about pushing your children toward specific paths, but about providing them with the tools and support they need to navigate their own journeys. Partners should be prepared to adjust their parenting roles and approaches based on their children's evolving interests and needs.

In the chapters ahead, we will explore the ways in which fostering individuality impacts various aspects of parenting, from education to decision-making. By nurturing the individuality of your children within the context of a supportive partnership, you help them blossom into confident, self-assured individuals who are empowered to pursue their dreams and contribute their unique gifts to the world.

10

Navigating Extended Family Dynamics

Harmonizing Bonds: Balancing In-Laws, Grandparents, and Parenting Choices

The canvas of collaborative parenting isn't limited to just partners and children; it extends to the intricate tapestry of extended family dynamics. This chapter delves into the delicate art of navigating relationships with in-laws, grandparents, and extended family members while making parenting decisions. It explores the ways partners can set boundaries while maintaining positive relationships that contribute to the overall well-being of the family.

Extended family members bring a wealth of love, experience, and support to the journey of collaborative parenting. However, differing viewpoints and approaches can sometimes lead to conflicts. Partners should first establish a united front by openly discussing their parenting goals and decisions. This sets the foundation for effective communication with extended family members.

When dealing with in-laws and grandparents, it's crucial to set clear boundaries while maintaining respect. Partners should have open conversations about the level of involvement they're comfortable with, the rules they've established for their children, and their expectations for family interactions. Communicate these boundaries in a loving and assertive manner.

Navigating extended family dynamics requires empathy and understanding. While you and your partner may have a shared vision for parenting, extended family members might have different perspectives. Approach these conversations with a willingness to listen and explain your choices, acknowledging that their advice comes from a place of love and concern.

Partners should be each other's strongest advocates when dealing with extended family dynamics. Presenting a united front reinforces that your parenting decisions are made as a team, based on mutual respect and shared goals. Address any disagreements privately and find solutions that align with your family's values.

Encourage positive relationships between your children and their extended family members. Grandparents and other relatives can offer unique insights, experiences, and traditions that enrich your children's lives. Maintain open communication, allowing them to feel valued and involved while ensuring that their role complements your parenting approach.

As a partnership, it's important to approach extended family dynamics with a sense of compromise. While certain traditions or practices might differ from your parenting choices, find ways to integrate them in a manner that respects both your family's values and those of your extended family members.

In the chapters ahead, we will explore how navigating extended family dynamics impacts various aspects of collaborative parenting, from holidays and celebrations to major life decisions. By creating a balance between setting boundaries and maintaining positive relationships, you enrich the tapestry of your children's lives with a diverse array of influences while maintaining the core values and goals that define your partnership.

11

Maintaining Intimacy as Partners and Parents

Kindling the Flame: Nurturing Romance Amidst the Roles of Parenthood

In the grand tapestry of collaborative parenting, the roles of partners and parents weave together to create a rich and fulfilling life. This chapter delves into the art of maintaining intimacy while balancing the roles of partners and parents. It explores how partners can nurture their romantic connection, carve out time for each other, and sustain the emotional bond that fortifies their partnership.

Amid the whirlwind of parenting responsibilities, it's essential to remember that the relationship between partners is the foundation on which your family stands. To maintain intimacy, make intentional efforts to keep the romantic spark alive. Engage in activities that remind you of the early days of your relationship, and continue to discover new ways to express your love and appreciation.

Balancing the roles of partners and parents requires thoughtful time management. Carve out moments in your day, whether it's through quick text messages, shared meals, or intentional conversations after the children have gone to bed. These small gestures reinforce the importance of your relationship and demonstrate that you remain present in each other's lives.

Partners should prioritize date nights and quality time together, just as they prioritize other aspects of their lives. Regularly schedule activities that allow you to focus solely on each other. Whether it's a night out or an evening in, these moments of connection remind you why you embarked on this journey together in the first place.

Maintaining emotional connection is vital for sustaining intimacy. Engage in open conversations about your feelings, dreams, and challenges. Share your experiences as parents and individuals, and be open to listening to your partner's perspective. By creating an environment of emotional vulnerability, you strengthen the bond that ties you together.

Children benefit from witnessing their parents' loving relationship. The partnership between parents serves as a model for healthy relationships, teaching them the importance of respect, communication, and compromise. When they see their parents nurture their love, they learn that love is not only expressed through parenthood but also through the partnership itself.

In moments of stress or conflict, remember that maintaining intimacy requires effort and understanding. Approach disagreements with empathy and respect, and find ways to resolve conflicts that prioritize your relationship while also considering the needs of your children.

In the chapters ahead, we will explore how maintaining intimacy impacts various aspects of collaborative parenting, from managing stress to decision-making. By nurturing your romantic connection and emotional bond, you lay the foundation for a partnership that not only thrives as parents but also flourishes as lovers. Through the roles of partners and parents, you create a symphony that harmonizes the beauty of partnership with the joy of parenting.

12

Growing Together as Parents and Partners

The Tapestry of Time: Reflecting on the Journey of Parenting as Partners

As the pages of the collaborative parenting journey turn, partners find themselves standing at the precipice of growth and transformation. This chapter delves into the process of growing together as parents and partners, inviting introspection and celebration of the shared experiences that have shaped your path. It explores the beauty of personal and relational growth and the excitement of looking to the future as a united team.

Reflecting on the journey of parenting as partners is an opportunity to acknowledge the milestones you've reached, the challenges you've overcome, and the moments of joy that have colored your days. Take time to revisit the goals you set, the strategies you employed, and the lessons you've learned along the way. Recognize the strength of your partnership and the resilience you've demonstrated as parents.

As partners and individuals, growth is a continuous process. Collaborative parenting invites personal development as you adapt to new roles, challenges, and responsibilities. Embrace the opportunities to learn from each other, acquire new skills, and evolve as individuals. The growth you experience as parents ripples through every aspect of your lives, enriching your perspectives and strengthening your bond.

While personal growth is integral, the growth of your partnership is equally significant. Celebrate the ways in which you've deepened your connection, strengthened your communication, and fostered a sense of unity. Every challenge faced and every triumph celebrated contribute to the tapestry of your shared journey.

Looking to the future as parents and partners involves setting new goals and envisioning the legacy you want to leave for your children. Discuss your hopes and dreams for your family, consider the values you want to pass on, and create a roadmap for the years ahead. By setting intentions and working toward shared aspirations, you ensure that your journey remains purposeful and inspiring.

As you navigate the uncharted territories of the future, approach it with the same collaboration and communication that have carried you this far. Embrace the uncertainties with a sense of adventure, knowing that your partnership and the skills you've developed as parents will guide you through whatever challenges arise.

In the chapters that have led you to this point, we've explored the intricacies of collaborative parenting, from communication and shared values to challenges and growth. As you reflect on this journey, let the tapestry of your experiences serve as a reminder of your strength, unity, and unwavering commitment to each other and your children. By embracing personal and relational growth, you ensure that your partnership continues to thrive, nurturing a legacy that will flourish for generations to come.

Conclusion: Embracing the Journey of Parenting as Partners

As we draw the final curtain on this exploration of collaborative parenting, let us take a moment to reflect on the key principles that have shaped our understanding of this transformative journey. From the concept of parenting as a partnership to nurturing individuality, navigating challenges, and maintaining intimacy, the threads of these principles have woven a rich tapestry of wisdom and insight.

At its core, collaborative parenting is a symphony of unity and partnership. It's the recognition that parenting is not a solitary endeavor but a shared commitment to raising our children in an environment of love, respect, and cooperation. By embracing the roles of partners and parents simultaneously, we create a harmonious balance that nurtures both our partnership and our children's well-being.

Effective communication emerges as the cornerstone of collaborative parenting. Through open and respectful dialogue, we bridge gaps, share perspectives, and build a strong foundation of understanding. The art of division of parenting roles ensures that responsibilities are shared, evolving with time and circumstances. Meanwhile, supporting each other's well-being keeps our partnership vibrant and strong, while fostering individuality empowers our children to flourish.

Facing challenges as a united team strengthens our bond and teaches our children the value of resilience and teamwork. By navigating extended family dynamics and maintaining intimacy, we enrich the family fabric with love, connection, and a sense of belonging. Ultimately, this journey of growth and transformation is an ode to partnership, empathy, and the unbreakable ties that bind us as a family.

Now, dear reader, as you close the chapter on these insights, I encourage you to take these principles and apply them to your own journey of collaborative parenting. Embrace the nuances of your partnership, communicate openly, and support each other's growth. Cherish the unique qualities of your children, navigate challenges together, and keep the flames of intimacy alive. Whether you're just beginning this journey or have been walking this path for years, remember that each day offers new opportunities to strengthen your partnership and enrich your family's story.

As partners, as parents, and as individuals, you have the power to shape your family's legacy. May your partnership continue to thrive, your children continue to flourish, and your love continue to shine brightly through the intricacies of collaborative parenting.

www.ingramcontent.com/pod-product-compliance
Lightning Source LLC
LaVergne TN
LVHW010442070526
838199LV00066B/6153